© Gina Allan 2003

ISBN 0-9550868-0-9

Bar Code: 9780955086809

Published by Gina Allan Publishing
P.O. Box 48
Kent
TN28 8WD

Tel/Fax 0870 794 1015

Web: www.GinaAllan.co.uk

E;mail: info@ginaallan.co.uk

Gina Allan Publishing

P.O. Box 48, Kent, TN28 8WD
Web:www.Gina Allan.co.uk email: info@ginaallan.co.uk
Tel/fax: 0870 794 1015

Books by Gina Allan:

Avoid the Pain Play the Game!
Sex and Money!
The Lovers Handbook!
Karma & Universal Laws!
Healing the Soul!
Tarot, Dreams & Symbol Interpretations!
Love Sex and Relationships!
Numerology & Astrology!

Intuition Cards! Designed by Gina Allan.

Factual Comical Books:

Body Fun Facts
The Male Anatomy, Know Your Man!
The Playboys Secrets Revealed!

Body Fun Fact Recorded Line 0906 507 2254

24 hrs Psychic Readings   0906 507 0414

Credit Card Line 08707 203 780

Know Your Man!

His Manhood!

The size and shape of a man's tackle is often compared to his masculinity and how capable he is, in operating in the world. Indicating the masculine qualities of the Macho, Assertive, Strong, Powerful man! Depending on the size and shape of his 'Tackle' will determine how much of these manly qualities he possesses!

With all these wonderful 'Macho Manly' qualities, we like, there needs to be room to balance out the Emotional side of his nature as well. Yes they do have emotions, if you know how to trigger them! This is the other bit, us girls want as well!
Now here is where the problem starts!

There are many different combinations that make a whole. 1/10th Macho, 9/10th Sensitive otherwise known as the Wimp! Or 2/10th Sensitive and 8/10th Macho, otherwise known as the Chauvinistic Pig!   Ideally we want two equal halves of 'Male' and 'Female' qualities making the perfect combination, of the 'Tough but Gentle Warrior', but as we know, that isn't quite the combination we get!

The 'Mans Tackle' is the CLUE to these varying degrees and combinations, whether it is just for show or they actually know how to use it!
This little book is filled with FACTS giving the Mans games away! The size and shape of the tackle reveals what their psyche contains, after all, that is where the males 'Brain Cells reside!

The Muscle Thick Penis

The wonderful 'Macho Man Type' with the muscled, sun tanned body, flexible muscles, with the 'Large Muscled Erection' to match!

A girl's 'Dream Guy' but soon becomes her 'Nightmare'!

Likes to show off and perform. Instant 'Physical' pleasure is what they seek and plenty of it!

As the Penis is the residence of the 'Males Brain Cells', a large 'Muscled Erection' normally means a large 'EGO'!

Flutter your eyelids and tell this guy how wonderful he is, and watch his head swell. The one in his trousers, that is!

In affairs of the heart they tend to use the 'Heart by Pass Route'. If they start to 'Feel the Emotions rippling' they 'Panic and Run'!

Their idea of a heart to heart is having sex with them on top of you, the hearts are closer that way!

That's why they have a large muscled chest to keep the heart safely locked away!

If you want any other form of 'Emotional' input, forget it. You can't get 'Blood from a Stone'!

The up side to the lack of 'Emotional Input' is that the 'Large Muscle Prick' is this size and shape because it gets exercised regularly. You want great 'Sex', then the chances are this 'Prick' would know what to do with it!

(Just don't expect to get anything else apart from a possible visit to the clinic!)

This type haven't quite got to grips with speaking from the heart, (they haven't found it yet) so most of the stuff they tell you is 'Bullshit'!

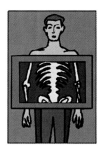

This guy's idea of 'Caring and Sharing' is sharing his body with lots of different girls!

Either together or individually!

The caring bit is that he cares that all the girls get enough of him and that his needs are satisfied!

So don't try and tell him, he's not a caring person, because he is!

This type of guy will have an abundance of friends and associates, all to keep his Ego topped up with feelings of being liked, admired, wanted and needed!

In other words he is very insecure!

The fact that they have an abundance of friends does indicate that they operate at a surface level, and are not ready for an INTIMATE relationship!

Which is why this type will be there as a shoulder to cry on or wave the magic wand. Talking of which 'Sex' always makes him feel better, it must do the same for you!

If you don't constantly feed his 'Ego' with meaningful wonderful words when you see him, he will be off to wave his 'Magic Wand' elsewhere!

This type will be found in the local 'Pub' or 'Clubs' where he will be sure to attract attention or of course working out down the 'Gym'. What better place to show off your muscles and get an Ego boost?

The Long Thick Penis

Well what can I say about this type? Apart from the word
'Thick' has more than one meaning here!

In fact the thickness of the Penis does indicate the type of
'Brain Cells' present! Muscle contains memory, indicating
the amount of 'Emotional Baggage' stored in the body
tissue!

But at least it is not all packed in tight and under tense control, like the 'Muscle Penis' who thinks with his muscles!

He is aware that he has feelings and has learnt that 'Fancy' words get him into more knickers, but he will keep his deeper feelings to himself. (Otherwise known as the Ostrich approach!)

This 'Prick' will use words of affection but just not in front of his friends. He needs to protect his 'Manly' image you see!

Which is why he will phone you regularly but he hasn't quite mastered the following up with 'Actions' bit yet! So get used to the 'Drip Feed System'!

This 'Prick' doesn't get quite the same physical work out as the 'Muscle Guy', but at least he does recognise he has a Heart!

Maybe doesn't know where it is or what you do with it but at least he is aware of having one!
(It's a start, there's something to work on!)

His conflict is between the Masculine side of being Strong and Manly and the Sensitive side of his 'Feelings' and 'Emotions'!

In other words he has a 'Jekyll and Hyde' approach to love. Now you see him, now you don't!
When the Emotions takes effect, he takes off!

The good news is, you know you have got to him!

The bad news is, it is more of a 'Fantasy' relationship rather than a physical one!

When you do have him in your crutches, his performance is a mixture of 'Making Love' and rampant 'Sex'!

The difference is in the degree of Emotions he is willing to show at the time!

So when you do 'Make Love' he will need time to have a 'Panic attack' for at least a week or two afterwards!

The Narrow Long Penis!

Again the word 'Narrow' has two meanings. They can be quite 'Narrow Minded' at times and like things done their way!

His Emotions tend to rule him more, rather than the macho image of showing off to friends!

He will use words to reinforce his feelings and likes to talk about meaningful things!

But as Emotions have a habit of causing tidal waves he can become quite irrational at times!

At least he has found his heart and is looking for a deeper form of 'Love' rather than just Sex!

Although 'Just Sex' does keep him interested and coming back for 2nds, 3rds, 4ths and 5ths in a short pace of time!

He has recognised the need to connect 'Mentally' 'Emotionally' and 'Physically' to have a lasting relationship!

This is the 'Romantic' type, long nights curled up in front of the fire or candle lit dinners together, speaking from the heart!

Yes this guy knows how to use his heart and will be the one for the Passionate Romantic Encounters!

But as the Heart is involved it is also vulnerable to pain
If you don't say the right words to him, he will crawl into
his shell and sulk for a while!

This type can be work-alcoholics. Their energy is more
Mental than Physical, so they like to do things that inspire
the 'Brain Cells' to work!

So the chances are if they are offered sex or their favourite
book, I am sorry but 9 out of 10 times they will go for the
Book!

At least you know he will be faithful physically, although he will like to flirt, making love to his mind!

As this 'Raising of Consciousness' moves the Brain Cells from below the belt line to above it, the blood rushes in the direction of the most Brain Cells!

To get him into a 'Sexy' mood you need to feed his mind first. Wear something sexy but leave things up to his imagination, get those Brain Cells working! Once you have his attention that sends the right signals to his Prick! (The one in his trousers)

Where do you find a guy like this?

Well he will be more into 'Marshal 'Arts', which involves disciplining the mind, also creative activities such as drawing/painting and artistic things. Most of the time you don't see them because they are already snapped up and 'Romancing' with their partner!

The Short & Dumpy!

As Muscle contains memory, he obviously suffers from
'Physical Memory Loss'!

In other words his forgotten what it is for!

His Brain Cells have had a 'Raising of Consciousness'
having made their way to the Head on his shoulders!

You now need to make 'Love to his Mind' before you get his Body!

Short & Dumpy will be more interested in talking about his feelings and connecting through closeness of cuddles. Physically, sexual techniques could be lacking, but he is the type to move forwards in a relationship with!

He will consider your feelings and do things to please you emotionally and physically. Whether that is what you want or not is a different matter!

Buying a dog will probably give you just as much satisfaction and be less irritating!

He can be stubborn, well moody really and a lot of the time he is absorbed in his own little Fantasy world in his mind and you would be surprised at what is in there!

If you want 'Sexual Pleasure' with him, you will have to make the first move and inspire to his mind first. Sex can be over in a flash if you let his mind wander. Keep it on the job in hand. Sexy words, moans and groans will help keep his attention Longer!

The Balls!

The Ball's contain the life force of a man, so the size and shape of them will determine how he deals with his Feelings!

Large full ball's indicates he knows what he wants, and stores his feelings up, only expressing them in a physical manor!
(In other words if he can't express it 'Sexually' he will want a Fight!)

The smaller Ball' s indicates he is being swallowed up by the Emotions. He finds them hard to deal with! Inwardly he is looking for something more 'Soul' satisfying rather than just a sexual encounter!

Feelings (firm balls) next to the prick (brain cells) is a
dangerous combination for a guy. It equals Love –
Relationship – Commitment - Marriage – Kids –
Mortgage – Divorce - Broke!

Emotions is what makes 'Sex' good. Ideally we want high
Loving 'Emotions' expressed through Sexual Activity,
We can all dream can't we!

Generally the Thick Pricks have the 'Sexual' experiences

The Short or Narrow ones have the Feelings!

If you want your cake and eat it, you have one of each!

Sadly, that doesn't give you the soul satisfaction but it can quench your thirst!

So it is down to you to give what your partner lacks, gently prompting him in the right direction! If the gentle approach doesn't work you can try the Domination and Humiliation approach!

If it is sexual activity he lacks, then Domination, Bondage, Whips and Toys will get that side going!

If it is a lack of 'Emotional Participation' then the Humiliation route works. Reminding him that by using the 'Heart by Pass' route, he is missing out on the full range of emotions!

Word Clues!

The Thick Pricks will use greetings such as 'Hun, Babe, Darling, Etc. The reason they don't use names is they don't want to call you by the wrong name accidentally!

Bear in mind their Mouth is at the opposite end of the body from the Brain Cells. His thoughts haven't quite got in to place before he speaks!

Affectionate words are a surface energy indicating that they operate via the 'Heart by Pass Route'!

As words are not their thing, they will give you just enough words to get in to your knickers then, that's your lot!

The Small & Narrow Pricks will give you all the words you want to hear, but the follow up with 'Sex' may be less exciting and takes some time to take off!

With the Thick 'Pricks Brain Cells' being below the belt line, meaningful words or conversations will be lacking and open for misinterpretation!

So when you ask him to make love to your mind, he will interpret this, as you want to give him a 'Blow Job'!

Unfortunately it seems that you either get all the Fancy Words (Mind) or the Physical pleasure (body), but to get the two together means the 'HEART' (Soul/Emotions) needs to be involved and that's the bit that men don't know they have!

The 'Brain Cells' reside either side of it!

Looks, Legs, Tit's & Bums

If you ask a man what he prefers, Looks, Legs, Tits or Bums this will give more clues to what he is looking for in a 'Perspective Partner'!

If he goes for Looks as the important factor, he only operates at a surface level. Instant sex and satisfaction is what he will want. The Dumb Blonde image comes to mind here, as she won't rock his 'Macho Lack of Confidence!'

If he prefers 'Legs' then it's a good indication that the 'Emotions' overwhelm him. He sees them capable of standing on their own two feet in the world, which invites security to him!

If he goes for 'Tit's' then he is really only looking for 'Sexual Encounters' nothing deep or lasting. An ego boost and sexual performance practise!

If he goes for 'Bums' it normally means he is looking for Ms Perfect! An inner cry, to get to the bottom of his insecurities and have a loving relationship!

Left or Right!

Regardless of what type the Penis is, you can tell if he has 'Sex for One' a lot and with what hand by the way the Penis bends!

If it bends to the 'Right' he obviously uses his right hand for the job, indicating he needs to get in touch with his masculine qualities of being assertive and put things into action!

(So put it down and get on with it!)

If it bends to the left, it is obviously his left hand he uses more, indicating that he needs to get in touch with his Feelings' and 'Emotions!'

If 'Percy' stands straight and tall then they have developed some kind of balance in their lives, 'Emotionally' and 'Physically'. They just need to put it into practise!

Body Hair!

Hair represents the 'Emotions' and is a form of psychological protection from the physical world!

Long hair - Sensitive, operates from the emotions, holds on to past issues, easily hurt, can be over emotional but operates deep from the heart!

Short hair – Surface energy, acts rather than feels, but has a level of confidence to operate in life!

Shaven head – Er – What emotions? No don't know what you're talking about!

Hairy Bodies & Tackle indicates they are more in tune with their feelings, the making love type rather than rampant sex!

Sexually they may long to live out their fantasies, but in practise their emotions hold them back, they are not that willing to experiment!

So have a book under the pillow, or stick a poster/mirrors on the ceiling to keep yourself amused!

Shaved or less Body Hair, especially around their Tackle and Anal area indicates a longing to overcome these Limiting 'Emotional Blocks'!

They act rather than feel,
So the emotions don't come in to it now!

But they are more than likely wanting and willing to experiment, having an exciting, varied and interesting sex life, in a bid to make up for the lack of emotional participation!

The Performers in life!

Techniques!

The 'Battering Ram' they use the full force of the hips to ram it in harder, they think you like it by your 'Moans and Groans'!

The Fact that you're Moaning and Groaning because it hurts, they haven't quite figured out yet! (Brain cells are in the wrong place!)

This technique is used by the 'Thicker Prick' so they can prove their 'Manhood' or maybe they are hoping for a 'Blow Job' at the same time!

The Smaller Dumpy Prick, have to ram it in harder for
obvious reasons!
(Try and humour them!)

The only difference between the two is 'Big Pricks' hurt
inside and outside, 'Small Pricks' only hurt on the outside,
but in either case they're all 'Pricks'!

As their Brain Cells reside above their shoulders or in their
trousers they haven't realised yet that it is what's between
the two heads that makes the difference to the QUALITY
of SEX!

That would be the 'HEART'!

Not how hard they can ram it in!

When the 'Heart' gets involved and that energy is
expressed through 'Physical Action' that's what
makes a 'Good Loving Relationship' and good
'SEX'!

Remember Lads, It is QUALITY that counts not
QUANTITY!

Pleasers or Not!

There are two types of men, ones that want to please and satisfy you and the ones that just want you to satisfy them by a quick 'Wam Bam Thank You Mam'!

Generally if they really like and want you, they will be eager to please, with 'Hours of long Foreplay' and 'Sexual' techniques!

(The Emotions are involved here & so is his 'Ego'!)

If however you only get quick 'Foreplay' and then they 'Shoot their Load,' it is pretty obvious you're wasting you time with them! (Indicates a lack of 'Emotional Participation'!)

So if your not happy with what you're getting, why stick around?

Pierced Pricks!

Apart from the image of going through something painful, therefore what a man he must be!

They will tell you it is for your pleasure and how good they can perform and turn a woman on!

However, all pierced parts indicates a deep lack of self-confidence within themselves to please or satisfy a partner. They think a lump of metal at the end of their prick will do the job for them!

So now we know why VIBRATERS were invented!

And

Why they are best sellers!